Unlocking the Secrets of Persistence and Success

By William T Gilbert

Unlocking the Secrets of Persistence and Success

By William T Gilbert

Disclaimer

The information contained in this book is personal research for educational and informational purposes only and does not constitute legal or other advice. Always seek help from a licensed professional before making any decisions. Any resemblance observed within this work to other works is purely coincidental as the content of this book was developed from personal research and input.

The publication is not intended as a source for legal, medical or accounting advice. The publisher wishes to emphasize that the information contained in this document may be subject to various international, federal, state and/or local laws or regulations.

The purchaser or reader of this publication assumes responsibility for the use of these materials and information. Compliance with all applicable laws and regulations, including international, state, federal, and any other aspect of doing business in the EU, US, Canada, or any other jurisdiction, is the sole responsibility of the purchaser or reader.

Neither the author nor the publisher assumes any responsibility or liability on behalf of the purchaser or reader of these materials. Any perceived offense by an individual or organization is purely unintentional.

This book is for personal use only. It is for reference only with no absolute guarantee of personal or financial gain. The result of using the materials described in this book depends on the use of this book.

TABLE OF CONTENT

CHAPTER ONE

The Great Renunciation in the Organization

The Great Renunciation

In a survey conducted recently, nearly 4.1 million American workers resigned from their jobs in October 2021 compared to July and August 2020. However, that was the lowest rate when 4.4 and 4.3 million people left their jobs. Perhaps, the exodus caused by the pandemic has triggered tectonic shifts in work culture. Workers have become more confident and are demanding for better benefits and wages and for more flexible working conditions. Somehow, companies chose to ignore employee resentment in favor of customer satisfaction, leading to a major upsurge.

Termination of an Employee

Employees are the ones who initiate the termination, or in other word, the resignation. They voluntarily decide to terminate their employment. Withdrawal is done by written notification, e-mail or letter. Do not forget about the notice period, which begins immediately after the employee has submitted the letter of resignation and ends on the last working day. While this may seem like a big deal, especially in many industries in the United States, it's not uncommon for companies to experience this phenomenon. This increase in resignations is mainly due to low-wage workers choosing higher-paying jobs. In most cases, they change industries looking for ways to onboard new employees as quickly as possible.

What Caused the Great Renunciation?
As economists have tried to explain, the Great Quit is closely linked to workers' dissatisfaction with their previous employment status. The ongoing global pandemic has prompted workers to reconsider their current status, long-term goals, work-life balance and working conditions. One of the main reasons employees quit in 2021 was that they were dissatisfied with the way employers were treating them during a pandemic. Also the lack of welfare they enjoyed and finally their inability to balance work and home life as many of them work from home.

It appears that workers in their 20s are more likely to quit than teenagers and older workers. Almost a third of workers in their 20s are leaving and changing jobs. Experts predict that this trend will continue into 2022 as people want to ensure more pleasant working conditions.

Common reasons for termination

a. They couldn't grow any more: professionals want to improve their skills and grow within a company. Yet the lack of opportunities seems to be one of the most common reasons for quitting.
b. They feel underpaid: Employees cannot accept that their colleagues at other companies are making more money, thereby realizing their market value.
c. They don't feel challenged: Great employees want to be challenged and involved in their work while seeking new learning opportunities. That is why companies need to arouse the interest of their employees.

d. They feel undervalued: Employees need recognition for their work. When an employer ignores your accomplishments, they look elsewhere for recognition and value.
e. They don't fit the corporate culture: Last but not least, this is perhaps the most difficult thing to fix. Fostering open communication is crucial if you want to retain your employees.

What is the large waiver?

ActiveCollab's report, Great Resignation has the potential to go far, but it's nothing we've never experienced before. The highest rates appear to be among workers in mid-career. Those between the ages of 30 and 45 show the largest increase in dropout rates. The percentage increased significantly by 20% in 2020 and 2021. In certain sectors, the healthcare and technology industries have seen the largest declines in the labor force. In particular, people who worked in these areas were more likely to suffer from burnout due to the increased workload.

Many economists assume that this is common. It's only natural for certain industries to experience employee turnover and we can't stop it. When we talk about the impact of the Great Waiver on the national economy, we have to admit that it does not have enough power to significantly disrupt market trends.

Why do employees quit their jobs?

The middle class led above all to dismissal. With so many of them working from home, companies have hired new employees who lack the necessary skills or personal training. Another factor we don't consider is the delayed transition. Perhaps this great resignation is the result of years of accumulated resignation. One could also assume that many employees have simply reached their breaking point. After months of intense and stressful work, many of them could no longer take the pressure and decided to quit. They want to rethink their work and life goals and maintain their sanity, which is the most important thing today.

Is the Great Renunciation still ongoing?

The Big Quit continued to make headlines in 2021. We've seen so many people leave their jobs, with a record number of employees leaving their jobs reaching a staggering 4.5 million in November 2021. The Great Renunciation led to the development of another term, the Great Reconfiguration, meaning that workers began to think about where, how, and why they wanted to work. They practically dealt with the role of work. In fact, it was a real moment of empowerment for many employees. Not only did they get another job; they took responsibility for their lives and made a big decision that would affect their entire career. Will this trend continue in 2022? It will, but the number of people leaving their jobs will be significantly lower. We will not see any significant changes in the labor market like in 2021. It is estimated that 23% of people will be looking for new job opportunities in 2022.

Employee Retention

If you want to keep your employees, you must first identify the source of their dissatisfaction. Conduct detailed analysis to understand what drives employees to quit. Try to find out if there are factors that compel employees to quit. It's important to look at the metrics. For example, the time between promotions, how much your salary has increased over time, your performance, have you given them any training opportunities, etc? In addition, it would be beneficial to segment employees by role, location, and other demographics to get better Understand how retention rates differ between employee populations. Companies need to develop specialized retention programs. Once you know why your employees are leaving, you need to start using highly customizable programs to fix specific problems.

CHAPTER TWO

The Elements of Toxic Work Culture

Toxic culture was the strongest predictor of attrition during the first six to 12 months of the Great Renunciation. It is 10 times more powerful than employee perceptions of their salary in predicting employee turnover.

By one estimate, employee turnover caused by a toxic culture was costing American employers nearly $50 billion a year prior to the Great Renunciation. Scholars have offered various, sometimes conflicting, definitions of toxic culture, and a cursory perusal of management writings and books revealed dozens of barely overlapping warning signs of toxic culture.

Employees complain about many things, but what elements of the culture are so awful that they're considered toxic? How can we tell a culture that's so horrible to be considered toxic by a culture that's just plain annoying? Identifying the elements that make a culture toxic is the first step in improving it. Leaders will waste their efforts and attention trying to improve all aspects of company culture that some employees find irritating. To understand what makes a culture toxic, you need to examine the language employees use to describe your organization.

Feeling disrespected in the workplace has the greatest negative impact on an employee's overall culture rating on any issue. Surprisingly, mentioning disrespect has a slightly larger negative impact on culture ratings than when an employee speaks directly and calls their culture toxic (or uses other extremely negative terms like "dystopian," "dumpster fire," or "sadness"). In other research, respect or lack thereof is the strongest predictor of how employees value organizational culture. This additional analysis shows that regardless of whether you look at culture at the individual employee level or aggregated within the organization, respect for employees tops the list of key cultural elements.

When employees join a company, they expect a culture that is inclusive, respectful, ethical, collaborative and free from abuse by those in power. When company culture fails to live up to these basic commitments, it's understandable that employees will respond with something stronger than anger or disappointment. In addition to the pain it inflicts on employees, a toxic culture also incurs costs that directly impact the company's bottom line. For example, if a toxic atmosphere makes workers ill, your employer usually foots the bill.

Companies with a toxic culture will not only lose employees, they will also have a hard time replacing employees who leave the ship. More than three quarters of jobseekers find out about the culture of an employer before applying. Almost half of employees who felt disrespected at work said they reduced their efforts and hours.

Even in the highest-rated companies, hundreds or thousands of employees can feel that corporate culture is toxic. For example, women, underrepresented minorities, or older employees may have a much more negative view of the culture than other employees.

Concrete steps leaders can take to detoxify their organizational culture is to encourage open communication if you want to keep your employees. Businesses need to develop specialized loyalty programs. If you only measure people by results, they will go to great lengths to avoid negative results. A pleasant work environment can have a direct impact on how employees fit in and how you can hire new employees. A positive work culture is a major competitive advantage. With the right culture, your business can go anywhere. Therefore, measuring company-level culture is a great way to identify factors that matter to many employees, such as: perks, benefits and job security. However, focusing on company-wide averages can miss elements of the toxic culture that are very important to a small percentage of the workforce. Therefore, for this book, we have looked at culture on an individual level.

To find out what poisons a company culture for employees, a study was conducted that focused on their negative feedback. The researchers use the text analysis platform developed by CultureX to identify topics that are discussed negatively by each employee. (The researchers measured a total of 128 subjects.) They then analyzed on a 5-point scale which of the above issues most negatively impacted employee ratings of organizational culture.

Grouping closely related elements into broader themes, the researchers identify the so-called Toxic Five attributes, which are disrespectful, non-inclusive, unethical, inconsiderate and abusive because they poison company culture in the eyes of employees. While corporate culture can disappoint employees in many ways, these five elements have by far the greatest negative impact on how employees perceive their culture and were the biggest contributors to employee attrition during the Great Renunciation.

The Toxic Five attributes (disrespectful, non-inclusive, unethical, inconsiderate, and abusive) have by far the greatest negative impact on how employees rate their culture in Glassdoor reviews. Each bar represents how little impact a negative mention of a topic had on an employee's assessment of culture. For example, if an employee says they don't feel respected when you rate them, their culture score will drop by an average on a five-point scale, all else being equal.

Here's how employees rate company culture in Glassdoor reviews:

Non Inclusive

According to the researchers' report, seven of the top 20 predictors of negative culture score relate to how strongly the culture at 500 companies encourages representation from diverse groups of employees and whether they are treated fairly, feel welcome, and will feel welcome in the decisions of workers' organizations involved. In general, this group of issues is the strongest predictor of employees who view their organization's culture as toxic.

The platform on whether organizations provide a fair and inclusive environment for specific demographic groups covers five themes: gender, race, sexual identity and orientation, disability and age. All of these identity issues belong to the top decile of the strongest predictors of a toxic culture.

Two other themes in the report capture comments about exclusion, which may or may not be related to demographics or an individual's identity. The theme of nepotism includes comments on nepotism and managers who play favorites, for example by promoting their friends or graduates of the same university instead of the most qualified candidates. The general non-inclusive culture theme includes criticisms that include terms such as "cliques", "clubby" or "in the crowd", indicating that some employees are excluded for no reason.

None of the diversity, equity and inclusion themes emerged as top predictors of an organization's overall culture in the researchers' analysis using collective employee ratings. This absence illustrates the danger of measuring corporate culture only in aggregate form. When leaders focus on examining the average employee culture, they may overlook issues that deeply affect a small number of employees. For example, in the report, respect is mentioned 30 times more often in employee reviews than justice, but both issues have the same impact on an employee's attitude toward culture when discussed negatively in the review.

Disrespectful

According to the researchers report, feeling disrespected in the workplace has the greatest negative impact on an employee's overall culture score on any issue. Surprisingly, mentioning disrespect has a slightly larger negative impact on culture ratings than when an employee speaks up directly and calls their culture toxic (or uses other extremely negative terms like 'dystopian', ' dumpster fire" or "sadness").

In another research, respect, or lack thereof, is the strongest predictor of how employees as a whole rate organizational culture. This additional analysis shows that whether you look at culture at the individual employee level or aggregated across the organization, respect for employees tops the list of key cultural elements.

Unethical

Ethics, like respect, is a fundamental aspect of culture that matters both at the organizational level and at the individual level. The topic of unethical behavior encompasses general comments about integrity and ethics within an organization. Common terms in the report associated with this topic are "ethical", "integrity", "unethical", "shady", and "scam". Under a related theme, dishonesty: employees described dishonest behavior in dozens of ways, including "lying", "cheating" and "making false promises", as well as related terms suggesting a concealment of the truth, like "smoke and mirrors." and "frosting."

Employees specifically addressed non-compliance with applicable regulations by their employer. Commonly cited regulations include Occupational Safety and Health Administration regulations, which protect worker safety in the workplace, and the Health Insurance Portability and Accountability Act, which protects confidential patient information.

Inconsiderate

Glassdoor Research Report commented on teamwork or collaboration. Employees often complained about uncooperative teammates or a lack of coordination across organizational silos. Coordination issues have a very modest impact on how employees perceive their culture. These banal frustrations are not necessarily red flags of a toxic culture.

Conversely, when employees talked about co-workers who actively undermined themselves, their comments strongly predicted negative cultural value. The 1% of employees who mentioned an unforgiving culture used descriptive vocabulary to describe their workplace, including "dog-eat-dog" and "Darwinian" and spoke of colleagues who "throw themselves under the bus", "stab each other", “back down” or “sabotage each other”.

Abusive

Abusive leadership is defining as persistently hostile behavior toward employees, as opposed to a boss having a bad day picking on team members.

The most frequently reported hostile behaviors are bullying, yelling or yelling at employees, belittling or belittling subordinates, verbally attacking people, and condescending or belittling employees.

According to the report, a third of employees said something about management in their rating, but only 0.8% described their manager as abusive. However, when employees mentioned abusive managers, the score was high.

When employees join a company, they expect a culture that is inclusive, respectful, ethical, collaborative, and free from abuse by those in power. These are not only basic elements of a healthy corporate culture, but also what companies often promise in their formal core values. In another research, "integrity," was cited by nearly two-thirds in companies as the most cited attribute among core business values, with collaboration as second, respect in fourth and diversity and inclusion in ninth place. When the corporate culture fails to deliver on these core commitments, it's understandable that employees react with something stronger than anger or disappointment.

The High Cost of a Toxic Culture

By identifying the core elements of a toxic culture, we can summarize existing research on closely related topics, including discrimination, abusive managers, and unethical behavior in organizations, workplace injustice and rudeness.

This research allows us to estimate the total cost of a toxic culture to individuals and organizations. And the cost in terms of human suffering and financial expense is staggering.

Numerous research results show that working in a toxic atmosphere is associated with increased stress, burnout and psychological problems.

Toxicity also leads to physical illnesses. When employees are treated unfairly in the workplace, their chances of being seriously sick (including heart disease, asthma, diabetes and arthritis) increases.

In addition to the pain inflicted on employees, a toxic culture also results in costs that directly impact the bottom line of the organization. For example, if a toxic atmosphere makes workers sick, their employer usually pays the bill. Among American workers receiving health care benefits, two-thirds of their health costs are paid directly by their employers. In 2008, toxic workplaces added an additional $16 billion to employee health costs, according to one estimate.

The below summarizes some of the costs of a toxic culture to business where staff turnover is higher.

A toxic company culture was 10 times more likely to attrition than reward in the first 6 to twelve months of The Great Renunciation where twenty percent of employees have left a job because of its culture. Replacing an employee can cost companies up to twice the employee's annual salary where a bad employer brand makes it harder to attract talent.

In another report, 73% of jobseekers in the United States only apply to a company if its corporate culture matches their personal values. According to a study by the Society of Human Resource Management, 1 in 5 employees quit a job at some point in their career because of their toxic culture.

Therefore, a toxic culture is the strongest predictor of a company experiencing a higher rate of employee disengagement in the first six to twelve months of Great Renunciation than its industry as a whole. Gallup estimates that the cost of replacing a departing employee can be up to twice their annual salary when all direct and indirect expenses are taken into account.

Companies with a toxic culture will not only lose employees but they will also struggle to replace employees who jump ship. More than three-quarters of job seekers research an employer's culture before applying.

A toxic employer brand makes it harder to attract candidates. The other costs of toxic culture are more difficult to quantify but can still add up. Extremely disengaged employees are nearly 20% less productive than their engaged colleagues because they try less and miss more days of work. Nearly half of employees who felt disrespected at work admitted to cutting back on their effort and working time.

Added to this is the risk of reputation. In another report, 85% of US CEOs and CFOs surveyed agreed that an unhealthy corporate culture can lead to unethical or illegal behavior. For example, after fraudulent sales practices at Wells Fargo were exposed in 2016, the bank paid billions of dollars in fines and lawsuits and saw its reputation as a company suffered the largest one-year decline in Harris Poll history.

Why Every Leader Should Care About Toxic Culture

You can think of a toxic culture as someone else's problem, confined to a handful of high-profile failures like Wells Fargo or the Weinstein Company, rather than something for your organization to worry about.

Unfortunately, culture toxicity is common. An average of 10% of American employees' at large corporations mentioned one or more elements of a toxic culture in the five years between 2016 and 2020. That means more than 6,000 miserable workers for the average large American company. Around this average there is a wide range from 2% to 22% of employees discussing toxicity in their culture. If 1 in 4 employees mention toxicity, it is correct to say that the culture as a whole is toxic.

What your corporate culture needs to be good

Even at companies with the highest Glassdoor ratings, hundreds or thousands of employees may believe the company culture is toxic.

For example, among representative minorities or older employees, women may have a much more negative view of the culture than other employees.

In most large organizations, disparate micro-cultures coexist within a single corporation, often across departments, functions, regions, or acquired companies.

Individual leaders also create subcultures within their extended team. Regardless of their origin, micro-cultures can deviate from the broader corporate culture, meaning even the best cultures can contain niches of cultural toxicity.

Concrete steps leaders can take to detoxify their organizational culture:

1. The first step, however, is to recognize that even the healthiest corporate cultures contain toxins.

2. Leaders should use thick segments (like roles or countries) to assess the culture at the level of individual leaders who, for better or for worse, create micro-cultures throughout the organization.

3. When measuring corporate culture, middle schools are so easy.

CHAPTER THREE

The Value Scales of a Toxic Work Culture

Every toxic workplace has its own unique fingerprint of unsavory personalities, questionable ethics, and silly regulations. There are no two narcissistic bosses or rule-obsessed HR departments are exactly alike in their horror. But according to some of the world's most savvy business commentators, beneath this surface diversity lies a surprising coherence.

Every toxic corporate culture is non-toxic in its own way. Some schools of thought argue that any sort of horrible corporate culture stems from a handful of fundamental flaws. A "toxic" culture isn't just a culture you don't like. Part of the confusion about what exactly constitutes a toxic culture, according to Hunter Walk, is that many of us use the term "toxic" casually to simply refer to a culture that doesn't appeal to us personally.

So, if a toxic culture isn't something idiosyncratic and individual that can be instinctively determined, how do you define when a company has a truly harmful or ineffective culture? Adam Grant provided a simple framework to answer this question in his Four Deadly Sins of Toxic Work Culture. He explained that the toxic corporate culture is always a lack of balance. Organizations become toxic when they drift too far on two competing value scales, which are relationships versus results and rules versus risk. To highlight each of these four 4Rs; your organization may be committing one of the four deadly sins of work culture:

Relationships - When a business isn't just about upsetting or upsetting people; it's no surprise that getting things done is low on the priority list. The result is mediocrity and a culture without accountability. "Even if you do a terrible job, you'll still be fine as long as people like you," Grant says of this first basic kind of toxicity.

Results - This is the other end of the trade-off between relationships and outcomes. On this side are the companies that value relationships so little that they throw human decency under the bus in the name of performance. Grant suggests that this type of toxicity is the deadliest sin of corporate culture and can lead to disrespect, abuse, unethical decisions, and reckless behavior.

Rules - Every company must balance the stability of the rules with the chances of the risks. If you stray too far from the rules, you end up with a bureaucracy that kills creativity and initiative. These are the companies that will ask you to submit triplicate forms just to use the restroom and will view even minor changes in the status quo with suspicion and hostility.

Risk - At the other end of the rule/bureaucracy spectrum is the utter chaos of anarchy without rules. When everyone can do whatever they want without coordination or alignment, people end up working one after another, valuable lessons are never learned, and a lot of effort is wasted.

"The code can be rewritten. Products can be built, modified, closed. Investors can be bought. And the culture discussion has to be very specific", Walk wrote on her blog.

Grant's framework provides a useful way to perform this type of assessment. Whether you're a job seeker trying to understand the culture of the company you might join, or an executive wanting to make sure job seekers don't see your culture as toxic, it helps to have a toxicity species mind map. You must be prudent. Grant's 4R offering is exactly that.

CHAPTER FOUR

The Danger of Toxic Work Culture

We all know that working for a company with a toxic culture is uncomfortable and stressful. But research on the effects of toxic workplaces remains woefully difficult to understand. A study found that a toxic workplace triples the risk of depression. Research also shows that firing a toxic jerk contributed more than twice as much to a company's bottom line as hiring a superstar. Another recent study found that a toxic job is the strongest predictor of employee compliance with the big renunciation. All of this should make it clear that you don't want to run (or work for) a company with a toxic culture. But this raises a simple but important question. What exactly makes a culture toxic?

We all have vague ideas about what kind of behavior counts as toxic, but recently a team at MIT tried to find a more scientific answer to this question. To find out exactly what caused toxicity levels to actually be achieved in a problematic work environment, the MIT research team analyzed 1.3 million Glassdoor reviews and used text analysis to determine which types of words and topics in the reviews had the largest reductions in represented a company Cultural value. Here are the top five signs of toxicity they spotted.

1. Rudeness and disrespect

Organizations in which employees complained that their colleagues lacked courtesy or were concerned about the dignity of others had a lower Culture Score on a five-point scale. Comments about disrespect were an even greater indicator of a poor Glassdoor culture rating than when employees used extreme language such as "dumpster fire" or "soul annihilation" in reviews.

2. Non-Inclusive Environment

Certain groups that are not welcome cost the company the talents of those excluded due to discrimination; it also seriously lowers the morale of those who join.

The team said a lack of full community involvement lowered average company ratings as much as general lack of courtesy, while differences versus people with disabilities and versus ethnic minorities lowered too. Several other types of injustice showed slightly smaller but still significant impacts, from age discrimination (scores decreased) to gender inequality and nepotism. This group of issues is the strongest indicator that employees view their organization's culture as toxic.

3. Unethical Conduct

Employees notice ethical shortcuts and they really don't like them. Unethical behavior lowered Glassdoor's company rating. The break led to a drop also. Reviewers used words like "shoddy", "cheater", "misleading", "making false promises", and "smoke and mirrors" to describe companies they felt were unethical.

4. Fierce competition

It can be tempting for managers to tolerate unsavory behavior in the quest for better performance, but this study suggests that in the long run they are likely to face severe penalties in terms of employee dissatisfaction and possible dismissal. Insidious behavior and fierce competition in a company lowered it's score.

Researchers are careful not to discuss shared territorial disputes or complaints about uncooperative colleagues. Instead, they point to companies where critics have used terms like "dog eat dog" and "Darwinian" to describe the culture, or have spoken of colleagues "jumping under the bus", "stabbing each other in the back", or " Sabotage each other".

5. Bullying

Not surprisingly, employees have no interest in being bullied or seeing their peers being bullied. Companies that have tolerated bullying, harassment, and other forms of open hostility have seen their results on Glassdoor review. Some of the most common problematic behaviors in this category are yelling at, putting down, swearing at, or humiliating others.

Fortunately, open bullying like this is relatively rare, but it has a major impact on culture. In their assessment, only insignificant figure identified their manager as abusive, the researchers reported. However, direct bullying may not be common, but researchers warn that toxic cultures are far from uncommon. Therefore, you might think toxic culture is someone else's problem, confined to a handful of high-profile companies and your organization doesn't have to worry. Unfortunately, cultural toxicity is common to all categories of company. So, if you're armed with this book, take a hard look at your own corporate culture and make absolutely sure you don't see any of these five hallmarks of a truly toxic culture.

CHAPTER FIVE

Rules for Measuring Success

One of the most important tasks of every leader is to define how to measure success. You've probably heard the phrase, “you get what you measure”. More importantly, you get what you reward. If you reward your team for their success, they will try to do more of what you gave them the reward for. So be careful what you measure and what you reward. If you get it wrong, your team will likely fail. Everything seems obvious, but in reality it is quite complicated. The reason is that the way most leaders define success misses one of the most important points.

In one report, an interview with Sundar Pichai , CEO of Google explained: "You have to encourage innovation...You know, one of the counter-intuitive things is that as companies get bigger, they become more conservative. You have a lot more money, you have a lot more resources, but companies tend to make more cautious decisions." As a result, Pichai says his job is to encourage the business to take risks, innovate and embrace failure, and to reward effort, not results.

The last part is really important. In fact, these four words are one of the most important lessons for any leader. As Pichai points out, this can be difficult because "people tend to reward results."

It is therefore important:

If you only measure people by results, they will do anything to avoid negative results. They play it safe and go with what they already know works. They will continue to give you exactly what you have always received, no more and no less.

Therefore, avoiding a negative outcome is not a good measure of success. Avoiding negative outcomes does not lead to greatness. On the other hand, if you want people to work really hard, reward them for it. If you want people to take risks, try new things, and find new ways, motivate them in their efforts.

These things don't always result in what we traditionally think of as success. Sometimes they are messy. Sometimes they fail. Sometimes the effort costs you a lot of money. That's not necessarily a bad thing when you're trying to build something new. If you try to do something worthwhile, you will often fail anyway. You will break things and figure out how to put them back together. It could also encourage people to learn from anything and reward them for their efforts. Of course, that doesn't mean you don't expect a lot from your team. That doesn't mean the results don't matter. It just means that the result you're looking for might be less obvious than a 5% year-over-year increase in your stock price.

It really depends on the type of culture and ultimately the type of business you want to build. If you want gradual growth and a small but steady increase in quarterly revenue, that's fine, but don't expect anything revolutionary to happen. However, if you want to build a team that's willing to do the hard stuff, reward them for their effort. Reward them when they try and fail and when they learn and succeed. In the end, that's the best possible outcome anyway.

CHAPTER SIX

The Best Explanation for Success

Google recently announced its results for the last quarter of 2021. Like many of its tech siblings, it was a very strong quarter. Google posted record revenue of $75 million, most of which came from the company's advertising business. In fact, Google's advertising business is so good that it loses money on everything else, but it still managed to post one of the most profitable quarters of any company. In the three months to December, Google made nearly $21 billion in profit. It's a way to measure success.

Undoubtedly, it is used by most companies and investors. For this reason, companies mostly host earnings calls to talk about what they sold and how much money they made. That's okay, because businesses certainly exist to make money.

However, during the company's earnings call with analysts, one phrase caught my eye: Google CEO Sundar Pichai used to summarize his findings.

"Our significant investment in AI technologies continues to enable exceptional and beneficial experiences for people and businesses through our key products."

Without going into too much detail, Pichai explained how Google uses artificial intelligence (AI) and machine learning to improve its products such as Maps, YouTube and search. Pichai spent several minutes talking about AI and how Google is progressing in this space, but that's not the interesting part.

Google says it exists to "organize the world's information and make it universally accessible and useful." It's not something a human can do. Your computer or smartphone cannot do this. Instead, massive amounts of dedicated machine learning and artificial intelligence are needed to understand the massive amount of information being created every second.

All that computing power is focused on one thing: helping Google deliver "extraordinary and useful experiences."

That's why Google is so successful. Of course, in terms of dollars, Google succeeds because it is the largest advertising platform in the world. But the reason why it is the largest advertising platform in the world is because billions of people find its services useful. It adds value to their lives by making it easier for them to find information.

Indeed, Google, like any other company, is focused on creating "extraordinary and useful experiences".

Think for a moment about how many Google services you use each day. Gmail is the standard email service for individuals and many small businesses. Google Search is what gets billions of people online for the first time. People use Google Maps to understand and navigate the world around them.

Google Maps is actually a great example. We rarely think things are amazing once they become the default, but I can't think of a better word to describe all the things you can do with Maps.

Not only can it tell you the best way to get from place to place, but you can also explore your destination right from the app. When you consider the amount of effort that goes into mapping and then photographing much of the world around us, Street View is truly remarkable. That's what makes it so useful.

I think that's actually a pretty compelling challenge for any business. If you think about it, your job is to do just that: create exceptional and useful experiences for your customers.

Even if you're not building the world's largest email service or the world's most visited website, you can still deliver something amazing. Often it's not just about building something better. Sometimes it's about the experience of buying or using your product or service. Sometimes it's the little things that no one else would think about.

Creating something ordinary is not a competitive advantage. Extraordinary and useful is the new standard expectation of your customers. It's also the best way to define success.

CHAPTER SEVEN

Improving Productivity in the Organization

Why do people quit their jobs? The pandemic has disrupted the way we work. Some employees are tired and want a renewed sense of purpose, belonging, and connection to people. Others want better pay, perks, and perks. In the meantime, the entrepreneurs among us want to take control, forge their own path, and put the new skills they learn to good use.

Today's workers expect more from their employers. They want flexibility, competitive pay and benefits, a positive work environment, and opportunities for advancement. During the Great Surrender, it is up to your organization to determine how to meet these changing expectations.

As an employer, understanding what employees are running away from can provide answers to stop the "big layoff" and attract new talent. Let's take a look at the challenges your business may be facing and ways to combat the big layoff.

Accept that work from home is here to stay. Working from home has become the new norm and a full return to the office is an unlikely scenario for many. In fact, it has been shown that workers are more productive at home and enjoy a better work-life balance. Working from home has become so popular that employees prefer not to take advantage of it.

In view of this trend and the hope for an end to the pandemic, hybrid forms of work are now becoming the norm. But many employers struggle to define what that means, and using a one-size-fits-all approach may not work. If you're thinking about changing your work-from-home policy, give it some more structure. Give your employees access to information and productivity tools that empower them while they're engaged.

Bring remote workers together with mentors outside of their department so they can have open conversations about their work and issues. Many companies have also found success with virtual coffee breaks or fireside chats, where teams can hold informal meetings that aren't work-related.

Be more strategic in meetings

Meetings can consume our days, limit productivity and increase stress. Research shows that hybrid employees who spend more time in meetings with their colleagues are almost 1.5 times more likely to be emotionally drained. Even more alarmingly, 40% of hybrid or remote workers report their workdays have grown longer over the past year, leading to more fatigue and burnout. What can you do? Consider limiting meetings to collaborative sessions, brainstorming sessions, or hands-on exercises. Anything that isn't urgent or is a one-page presentation (e.g. business updates) can be saved for another time or format. Also, limit the guest list to those who are expected to actively contribute. Even if action is needed from those not present, share a recording or give them an offline update.

Support professional development

The prospect of professional advancement is an important bonding factor. A Harvard Business School poll found that 62% of workers believe professional development, including professional training and certification, is important. Don't limit training to classroom or online classes, however. Invest in mentors and career paths that give workers a clear picture of what it takes to advance their careers. Set clear milestones and set up resources and support that can help them get where they want to be.

Hands-on career development, exposing employees to new ventures or expanding beyond their job description, can also be helpful. However, beware of expanding the scope of work and increasing your workload.

Have an authentic organizational purpose

McKinsey research shows that 70% of people define their purpose through work. This is especially true for millennial, who tend to see work as their calling in life. When you help your employees find meaning at work, they're more likely to stay, perform better, and contribute to the success of your organization.

How do you develop and share an authentic company purpose? Consider the role your company plays in today's turbulent and changing world and society. Don't just think about your community and your causes, think about the impact of your company's mission, actions, and brand, and spend time reflecting with your employees.

Money is always important

Money is one of the engines of the Great Renunciation. Faced with demand for talent, employees are quitting their jobs and looking for new opportunities that offer sign-on bonuses and a raise, rather than staying where they are and doing the same work for less. Rather than diminishing your bottom line, offering an attractive salary can pay off. When you succeed in attracting and retaining talented employees, they can have a significant and positive impact on the future of your company.

Take corporate culture seriously

Work culture is the main point to stemming the tide of the Great Renunciation. A pleasant work environment can have a direct impact on how well employees fit in and how you can recruit new employees. In fact, experts say that a positive work culture is a great competitive advantage. James L. Heskett, UPS Foundation Professor Emeritus at Harvard Business School, says that an effective corporate culture leads to stronger employee and customer retention and loyalty, which translates to increased growth and profits. With the right culture, your business can go anywhere. After all, it's easier to change a strategy than a culture.

CHAPTER EIGHT

Conclusion

Company culture is not something you write in the employee handbook and expect everyone to adopt. When it comes to corporate culture, many business owners, especially those who have not been in business very long, will dismiss corporate culture as a big business issue. Believe it or not, your company has a culture. It's up to you to shape this culture in a way that not only benefits your team members, but also the growth and development of your company as a whole.

You have to remember that your organizational culture is reflected in the questions people ask or don't ask about how they do or don't behave. Maybe you have a habit of always being too nice when it comes to having difficult conversations. Perhaps you are very good at doing what you say. Perhaps you have a habit of treating new team members a little coldly until they prove themselves? Maybe your team is great at celebrating victories within the company. Either way, good or bad, it's part of what makes your business successful (or unsuccessful).

Corporate cultures do not develop overnight. It's not something you write in your employee handbook and hope everyone adopts. Company culture is created as small behaviors, events, stories and hammer blows slowly accumulate, so to speak. Which fittings would make a difference in your own business? Do you share success and failure stories in learning together as a team? Do you lead by example? Do you celebrate victories? Do you empower team members to take responsibility for their success? Do you train employees for growth? Whatever you think will change your business over time, write it down. Think about how you can make small touches every day because over time those touches make a difference. What if your management team did the same? Suddenly, your little details and those of your leadership team morph into something much bigger.

The biggest indicator of success in creating and shaping a corporate culture is habits. We are all busy and have a thousand things on our plates. It's so easy to make a list of ideas that we think are important to our culture, but it's much more important to make a habit of working with them every day when you put them on your To-do list must be set. Create a spreadsheet or journal that you write in daily and stand up for it. After a month it becomes a habit. After a year, you won't remember a time when you didn't do the daily or weekly hammer hits, and that's where the magic happens.

www.ingramcontent.com/pod-product-compliance
Lightning Source LLC
LaVergne TN
LVHW052109160826
845678LV00015B/3456

* 9 7 9 8 8 4 1 4 2 4 0 3 1 *